HIDDEN BLACK HISTORY
From Juneteenth to Redlining

Amanda Jackson Green

Lerner Publications ◆ Minneapolis

Content consultant: Dr. Artika R. Tyner, President and CEO of Planting People Growing Justice

Lerner Publications Company
An imprint of Lerner Publishing Group, Inc.
241 First Avenue North
Minneapolis, MN 55401 USA

For reading levels and more information, look up this title at www.lernerbooks.com.

Library of Congress Cataloging-in-Publication Data

Names: Green, Amanda Jackson, 1988- author.
Title: Hidden Black history : from Juneteenth to redlining / Amanda Green Jackson.
Description: Minneapolis : Lerner Publications, [2021] | Series: The fight for Black rights | Includes bibliographical references and index. | Audience: Ages 8–12 | Audience: Grades 4–6 | Summary: "From Juneteenth to the Tulsa Race Massacre, many important moments in Black American history have not been taught in schools or covered in the media. Discover these events and how they are remembered in the Black community today"—Provided by publisher.
Identifiers: LCCN 2020041890 (print) | LCCN 2020041891 (ebook) | ISBN 9781728429588 (library binding) | ISBN 9781728430287 (paperback) | ISBN 9781728429632 (ebook)
Subjects: LCSH: African Americans—History—Juvenile literature. | African Americans—Historiography—Juvenile literature. | African Americans—History—Study and teaching—Juvenile literature. | African Americans—Anniversaries, etc.—Juvenile literature.
Classification: LCC E185 .G754 2021 (print) | LCC E185 (ebook) | DDC 973/.0496073—dc23

LC record available at https://lccn.loc.gov/2020041890
LC ebook record available at https://lccn.loc.gov/2020041891

Manufactured in the United States of America
4-51984-49523-10/13/2021

Table of Contents

CHAPTER 1

1619 4

CHAPTER 2

Teaching Black History 10

CHAPTER 3

History Remembered 16

CHAPTER 4

New Lesson Plans 24

Hidden Black History Timeline 28

Glossary 30
Learn More 31
Index 32

CHAPTER 1

1619

Leaders from around the Virginia colony gather in Jamestown on June 30, 1619. It is the first time the men have gathered in one place. They are there to form the colony's first government.

A few weeks later, a ship called the *White Lion* arrives in Virginia. The ship's captain brings about twenty enslaved Black people with him. They had been kidnapped from their homes in West Africa by a Portuguese trader. They were then stolen by the crew of the *White Lion*. The ship's crew needs food and supplies. The captain makes a deal with the colonists. He will trade the enslaved people for the items he needs.

The colonists agree. They force the enslaved people to work in their homes and to tend their crops. This marks a key moment in the history of slavery in the United States of America.

Historians believe the first enslaved people in the British colonies were from what is now Angola, a country in southwestern Africa.

UNFAIR SYSTEMS

The Founding Fathers added the Bill of Rights to the US Constitution in 1791. It was a list of rights that protected citizens. But only white men who owned property were considered citizens. The laws did not protect Black people from unfair treatment.

When the Constitution was written, it did not include rules about who was allowed to vote. For many years, only white men had the right to vote in most states.

Until the mid-20th century, Black people in the South were required to use separate water fountains, restrooms, and swimming pools.

Laws and policies that lead to or uphold racial inequality are known as systemic racism. Slavery and Jim Crow laws are two examples of systemic racism. Many of the systems that were built to reinforce racial inequality still exist today.

Historians argue that systemic racism is a major issue in the public education system. Some say the way history is taught is harmful to Black people. They believe that there is a better way to tell American history. They want to show how Black people have shaped the US from 1619 to the present day.

UNTOLD HISTORY

History is a collection of stories about past events. Societies decide which stories are important and how to pass their history to future generations. Many Indigenous peoples, such as the Inuit Nations and the Seminole Tribe of Florida, share history through oral tradition. Enslaved Black people shared their own oral histories. Colonists mostly used writing to record their stories.

Enslaved Black people adapted traditional folktales to share their own stories of survival, hope, and the possibility of freedom.

Benjamin Franklin *(left)* and the Founding Fathers made decisions on behalf of all citizens, including enslaved Black people.

From the nation's founding, white people decided which stories to tell as part of American history. Early historians valued written history over oral history. They preferred stories that focused on white people and their actions. Often, these histories left out or lied about harmful things white people did. Historians rarely recorded stories about Black or Indigenous people. This kind of biased storytelling is called whitewashing.

? Have you ever listened to someone tell a story? How is it different from reading a story? Do you prefer one or the other? Why?

CHAPTER 2

TEACHING BLACK
History

In 1926, Carter G. Woodson created Negro History Week. He wanted more people to learn about Black history. He chose the second week in February to celebrate the birthdays of two important figures in Black American history: Abraham Lincoln and Frederick Douglass.

During the week, people shared stories about Black people and their achievements. Community organizers taught lessons at schools and public events across the country. Churches, schools, and other civic organizations also held public events to celebrate Black culture.

Over the next several decades, Negro History Week grew in popularity. In 1976, President Gerald Ford declared February Black History Month in the United States. Americans still celebrate Black History Month each year.

The NBA celebrated Black History Month in 2020 with performances, pregame activities, and limited-edition gear. Miami Heat forward Jimmy Butler wore a special T-shirt for warm-ups.

ONE NATION, TWO HISTORIES

Black History Month helped bring more attention to the stories of Black people. However, many schools teach Black stories only in February. These lessons are often limited to certain periods, such as the Civil Rights Movement.

Black stories are often told separately from stories about white people. Often, they are not included at all. For example, history lessons often focus on white soldiers who fought in the Civil War. But students rarely learn about the almost 180,000 Black soldiers who served in the Union army.

During the Civil War, Black units were not used in battle as much as white units, due to prejudice and discriminatory practices.

Sometimes, lessons completely skip over the achievements of Black people. Science textbooks often leave out the stories of Black scientists such as astronaut Mae Jemison and inventor Otis Boykin. In 1992, Jemison became the first Black woman to go to space. Boykin created more than twenty-five inventions, including an important improvement to the pacemaker.

Hidden Figures

Hidden Figures is a movie about Katherine Johnson, Dorothy Vaughan, and Mary Jackson. They were three Black scientists working at NASA in the 1960s. NASA wanted to send an astronaut named John Glenn into Earth's orbit. They needed to solve very difficult math problems to do it. They did not have computers like the ones we have today. The three women worked together to solve the problems with calculators and rulers. Their plan worked, and John Glenn had a safe trip to space. It was the first successful mission to send an American into orbit.

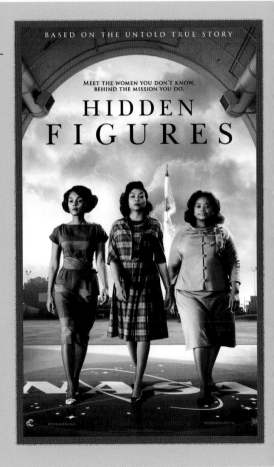

GAPS IN LEARNING

Most children in America attend public schools. State governments decide what public schools must teach. This includes which stories teachers must include in history lessons. Americans' understanding of history can vary by state. Students in Maine may learn different things from students in Texas, for example.

Although Black people have been a vital part of US history, many children only learn about Black Americans during Black History Month each February.

Dr. Martin Luther King Jr. *(center)* was a vocal advocate of protest as a **tool for change.**

The way Black stories are told can vary greatly from state to state. Seven states do not mention slavery in their education standards. Other state standards do not mention the Civil Rights Movement. Many teachers do teach these subjects. However, each teacher's lesson may be different. This can create large gaps in what people know about Black history.

Some Black history lessons tell only one side of the story. For example, many classes study the "I Have a Dream" speech Martin Luther King Jr. delivered at the March on Washington on August 28, 1963. Lessons often focus on King's vision of freedom and unity. They often exclude his criticism of police brutality, segregation, and injustice.

?

History lessons often leave Black people out. Have you ever felt like your voice wasn't being heard? How did it make you feel?

CHAPTER 3

HISTORY
Remembered

Many Americans connect the idea of freedom to Independence Day. This was the day in 1776 when the US declared its freedom from British rule. Other Americans link freedom with the Emancipation Proclamation of 1863. This was when President Abraham Lincoln ordered Southern states to free enslaved people.

But the Emancipation Proclamation did not free all Black people. The Civil War was still going on. The South was fighting to keep Black people enslaved. Most Southern slaveholders did not follow the order. As Union troops gained control of Southern land, they brought the news of freedom to enslaved people.

The Civil War ended in April 1865. On June 19, General Gordon Granger brought the news of freedom to Black people in Texas. Finally, freedom had arrived for all enslaved people in the South. The next year, Black Texans celebrated their freedom. They called the holiday Juneteenth. Today, Juneteenth is an official holiday in forty-seven states.

Local leaders and citizens of Chicago gathered on Juneteenth in 2020 for a march to celebrate Black rights and call for an end to systemic racism.

The Tulsa Race Massacre lasted for two days and left nearly ten thousand people without homes.

THE ROARING TWENTIES

The 1920s are often described as a happy time in America. The decade is called the Roaring Twenties because it was a period of economic and cultural growth. People earned more money. Cities grew. Jazz music and dancing became popular. The Nineteenth Amendment granted women the right to vote.

The Roaring Twenties were also a time of racial tension in America. White Southerners created Jim Crow laws to limit Black people's freedom. The laws enforced segregation and restricted Black people's rights to vote, get married, and hold certain jobs. Lynchings became a common way to make Black people live in fear.

In 1921, white mobs killed as many as three hundred Black people in Tulsa, Oklahoma. They destroyed thousands of homes and businesses in the Greenwood District, a wealthy Black neighborhood known as "Black Wall Street." In the years that followed, Tulsa newspapers and police departments destroyed and hid records of the incident.

The Harlem Renaissance

In the 1920s and 1930s, thousands of Black people moved from rural towns in the South to big cities in the North, Midwest, and West. This relocation is known as the Great Migration. Many Black writers, artists, actors, and musicians lived in Harlem, New York. They used songs, poems, books, and paintings to tell stories about their lives. The artists spoke out against racism and taught others about Black culture. This social movement is known as the Harlem Renaissance. Some of its leaders included Langston Hughes, Zora Neale Hurston, and Aaron Douglas.

Langston Hughes

THE CIVIL RIGHTS MOVEMENT

The Civil Rights Movement of the 1950s and 1960s is a well-known era of Black history. Martin Luther King Jr. and Rosa Parks are famous civil rights leaders. However, there were many other important leaders in the fight for justice.

Rosa Parks was arrested for her participation in the Montgomery bus boycott.

Fannie Lou Hamer helped found the Mississippi Freedom Democratic Party because there were no Black people representing Mississippi at the Democratic National Convention.

One lesser-known leader was Fannie Lou Hamer. In 1962, white poll workers denied her right to register to vote because she did not pass a literacy test. The tests were a common way to block Black people from voting. Hamer worked hard to change this unfair treatment. In 1964, she helped organize Freedom Summer, a series of events to help Black Southerners register to vote. She also organized protests and gave speeches about the importance of voting. In 1969, she launched the Freedom Farm Cooperative, which helped more than three hundred Black families buy land and start their own businesses. The organization also built two hundred homes for low-income families in Ruleville, Mississippi, many of which still exist today.

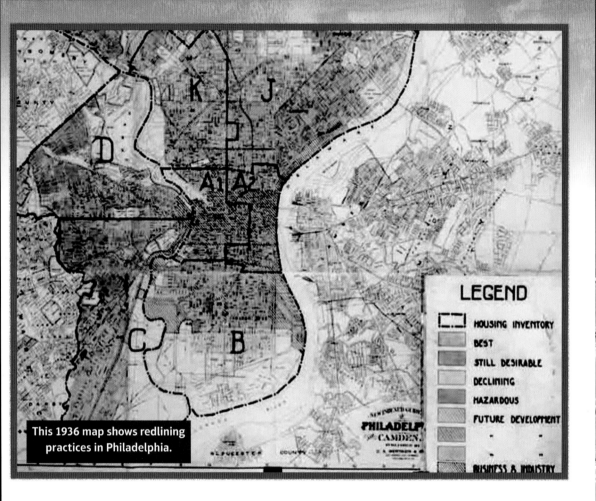

LEGEND

HOUSING INVENTORY
BEST
STILL DESIRABLE
DECLINING
HAZARDOUS
FUTURE DEVELOPMENT
BUSINESS & INDUSTRY

This 1936 map shows redlining practices in Philadelphia.

LATE 20TH AND EARLY 21ST CENTURY

The fight for Black rights did not end in the 1960s. Unfair laws and policies continued to create barriers to equality even after the Civil Rights Movement.

Banks often denied loans to people who lived in Black neighborhoods. This practice is known as redlining because lenders often used red ink to define these areas on a map. Redlining was outlawed in 1968. But by then, most homes were owned by white families. They were able to increase their wealth by selling the homes they purchased during redlining. Many Black families could not afford to buy a home.

Redlining is just one example of the ways Black people continued to be treated unfairly. Today, organizations like the National Association for the Advancement of Colored People (NAACP) are carrying on the fight for social, economic, and educational equality for all Americans.

Black people in America continue to fight for basic rights and equal treatment under the law more than fifty years after the Civil Rights Movement.

? The Fifteenth Amendment gave Black [...] vote. Still, they were sometimes bloc[...] Why is voting important?

CHAPTER 4

NEW LESSON
Plans

The events of the past affect the present. Leaders in the past made choices that impact people living today. Learning history can help people understand these connections.

In 2020, a Black man named George Floyd was killed by police in Minneapolis. He was accused of using fake money at a store. A police officer handcuffed him and restrained him with a choke hold. Floyd told the policeman he could not breathe. However, the officer would not release his grip. Floyd stopped breathing and died a short time later.

People angry about Floyd's death organized protests in all fifty states. Activists compared his death to the lynchings of the 1920s. They argued that systemic racism was still harming Black people. They believed that everyone should know the struggles of Black history. Many educators say that learning Black history can help Americans recognize and change unfair laws, policies, and systems.

Black Lives Matter murals and messages sprang up across the US in the weeks after George Floyd's death. They brought attention to issues of racism and inequality in America.

LIFTING UP BLACK VOICES

Educators have pushed to include more Black stories in history classes. For many years, Texas textbooks did not include slavery as the main reason for the Civil War. Many accused Texas of whitewashing. In 2015, Texas announced that textbooks would no longer refer to enslaved people as workers and immigrants. Texas history lessons were updated again in 2018. They now teach that the Confederacy's main goal was to continue slavery. By 2020, some Texas high schools offered an entire class on Black history.

There are nearly two hundred public symbols of the Confederacy in the state of Texas, including many large monuments and statues.

Ava DuVernay is the first Black woman to direct a film with a $100 million budget and the first to direct a movie that earned $100 million at the box office.

Art is another way to share Black history. Ava DuVernay is a writer and director. She uses her shows and movies to lift up Black voices. Her film *13th* explains how systemic racism led to more Black people in prisons. Kenya Barris is another Black director. His TV show *Black-ish* connects Black history to the present. The show covers topics such as voting rights, Juneteenth, racism, and whitewashing.

? Books, TV shows, movies, and music play important roles in teaching Black history. Why do you think art is a good way to share stories?

HIDDEN BLACK HISTORY
Timeline

August 20, 1619: The first enslaved Black people arrive at the Virginia Colony.

June 19, 1865: The last enslaved people in Texas learn they are free.

June 19, 1866: Black Texans celebrate the first Juneteenth holiday.

1920s: Artists in Harlem create works that celebrate Black life. The movement is called the Harlem Renaissance.

May 31–June 1, 1921: White mobs kill up to three hundred people in the Tulsa Race Massacre.

February 7, 1926: Carter Woodson creates Negro History Week.

February 20, 1962: Black scientists Katherine Johnson, Dorothy Vaughn, and Mary Jackson help NASA launch John Glenn into space.

June 15, 1964: Fannie Lou Hamer begins her efforts to register Black voters. This project is called Freedom Summer.

1964: Otis Boykin invents new parts that improve the pacemaker.

February 10, 1976: President Ford declares February Black History Month.

September 12, 1992: Astronaut Mae Jemison becomes the first Black woman in space.

May 25, 2020: George Floyd is killed by police in Minneapolis. His death sparks protests against systemic racism in all fifty US states.

Glossary

activist: someone who works to make change in the world

biased: having an often unfair preference for certain ideas, groups, or individuals over others

choke hold: the use of force to block a person's airway, restricting their breathing

Jim Crow laws: laws used post-Reconstruction to take away the rights of Black people

literacy test: a test of reading ability that a person must pass in order to vote

lynching: a killing, most often by hanging, of a person by a group without due process

oral history: the passing down of culturally important stories and historical events through word of mouth

segregation: the forced separation of different racial groups

systemic racism: patterns and policies that enforce discrimination based upon race

whitewashing: emphasizing the role and importance of white people while downplaying or ignoring the role and importance of people of color

Learn More

Black History Month: National Geographic Kids
https://kids.nationalgeographic.com/explore/history/black-history-month/

Harlem Renaissance: Britannica Kids
https://kids.britannica.com/kids/article/Harlem-Renaissance/353232

Mangal, Mélina. *The Vast Wonder of the World: Biologist Ernest Everett Just.* Minneapolis: Millbrook Press, 2018.

Norwood, Arlisha. *Black Heroes: A Black History Book for Kids: 51 Inspiring People from Ancient Africa to Modern-Day U.S.A.* Emeryville, CA: Rockridge Press, 2020.

Schwartz, Heather E. *NASA Mathematician Katherine Johnson.* Minneapolis: Lerner Publications, 2018.

Slavery: Ducksters
https://www.ducksters.com/history/colonial_america/slavery.php

Index

Black History Month, 10, 11, 12, 14, 29

Civil Rights Movement, 12, 15, 20, 22, 23

Civil War, 12, 16, 26

DuVernay, Ava, 27

Emancipation Proclamation, 16

Hamer, Fannie Lou, 21, 29
Harlem, New York, 19, 28

Jim Crow laws, 7, 19
Juneteenth, 16, 17, 27, 28

King Jr., Dr. Martin Luther, 15, 20

National Association for the Advancement of Colored People (NAACP), 23

Parks, Rosa, 20

redlining, 22, 23

slavery, 4, 5, 7, 8, 9, 15, 16, 26, 28
systemic racism, 7, 17, 24, 27, 29

Tulsa Race Massacre, 18, 19, 28

voting, 6, 18, 19, 21, 23, 27

whitewashing, 9, 26, 27
Woodson, Carter G., 10, 28

Photo Acknowledgments

The images in this book are used with the permission of: Hulton Archive/Getty Images, p.5; Mike Flippo/Shutterstock, p.6; FPG/Getty Images, p.7; Internet Archive Book Images/Wikimedia, p.8; Rischgitz/Hulton Archive/Getty Images, p.9; Brian Rothmuller/Icon Sportswire/Newscom, p.11; MPI/Getty Images, p.12; Levantine Films/Entertainment Pictures/ZUMA Press/Newscom, p.13; monkeybusinessimages/iStockphoto/Getty Images, p.14; Pictorial Parade/Getty Images, p.15; Antwon McMullen/Shutterstock, p.17; JT Vintage/Glasshouse via ZUMA Wire/Newscom, p.18; Hulton Archive /Getty Images, p.19; Adam Cuerden/ Associated Press/Wikimedia, p.20; Warren K. Leffler/U.S. News & World Report Magazine/Wikimedia, p.21; Mattho69/Wikimedia, p.22; Dustin Chambers / Getty Images, p.23; Stephanie Keith/Getty Images, p.25; Andre Jenny Stock Connection Worldwide/Newscom, p.26; Alberto E. Rodriguez/Getty Images, p.27; rosiekeystrokes/Pixabay, background

Cover: NASA (restored by Adam Cuerden)/Wikimedia, left; N. Flayderman & Co./ The Supervisory Committee For Recruiting Colored Regiments/Wikimedia, middle; Bastiaan Slabbers/Getty Images, right